# LETTER FROM THE EDITORS

Through the words and works of our LGBTQ+ friends, we hope to have been able to create a space where love can shine through and where acceptance can thrive. Systematic oppression may try to have and hold us, but the fight for equality can only continue so long as we stand together. We fight for all those around the world who came before us and who died not being free. We fight for ourselves and for each other in the hopes that we do not have to suffer the same fate.

This is our good fight, for love.

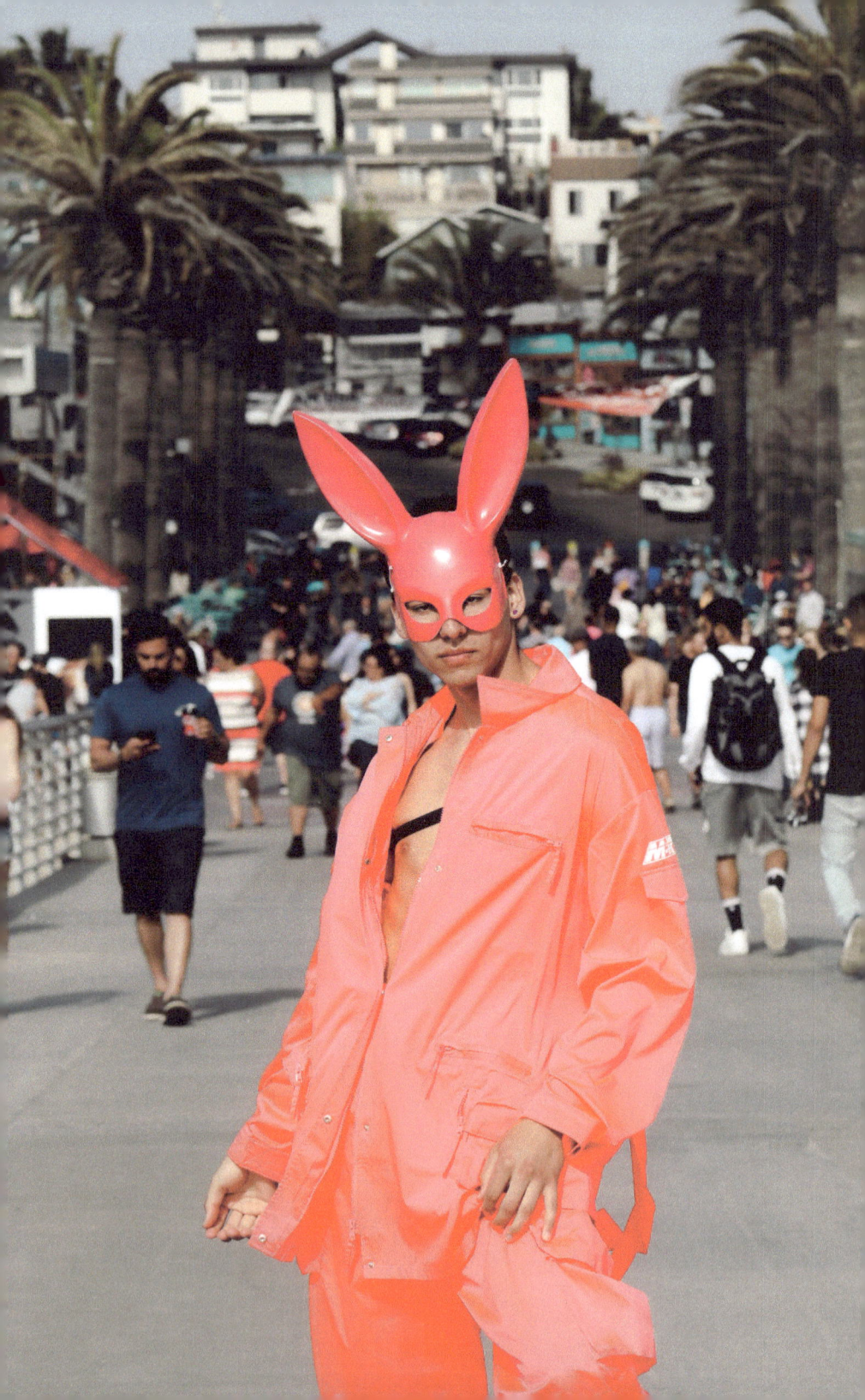

**EDITORIAL SHOOT**
Photographer: Josephine Jael Jimenez
Model: Jacquex Frankel

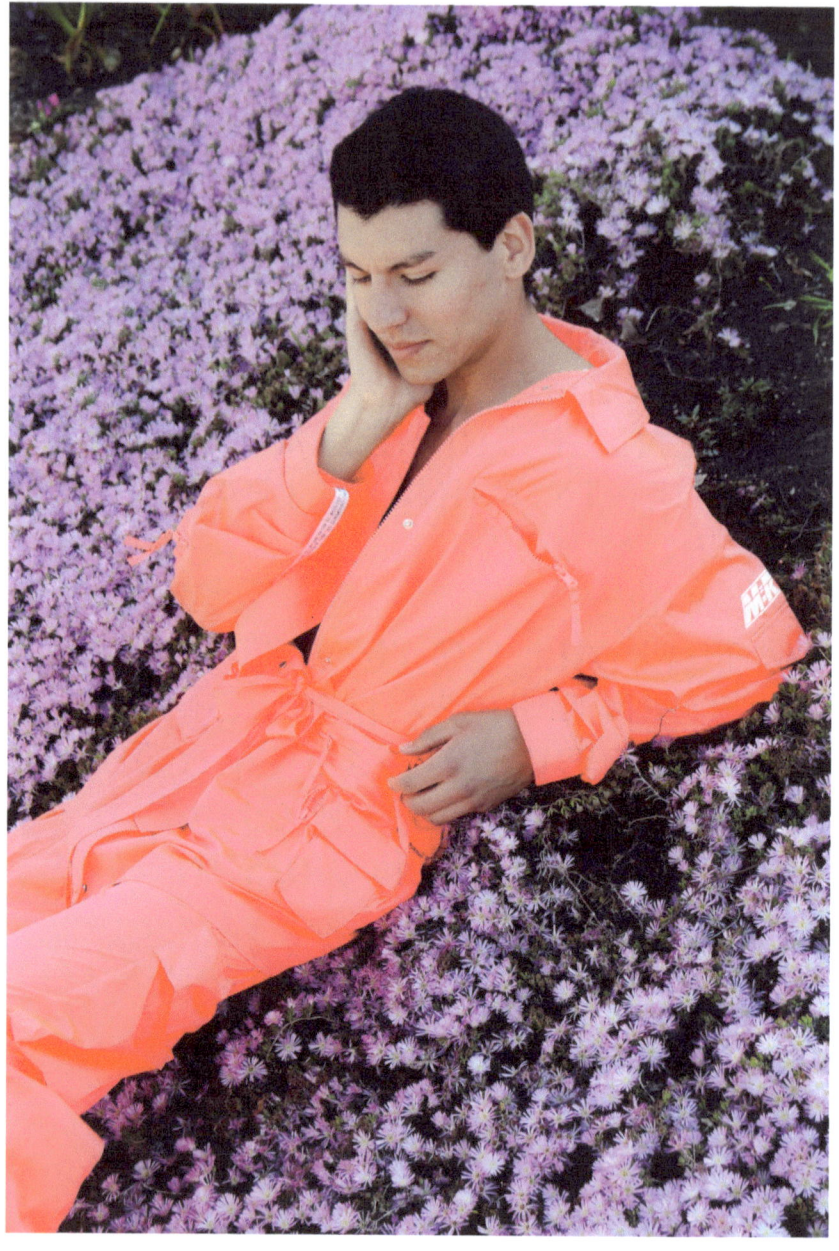

# The Power and Beauty
# of Being Jacquex

Text by Brenda Hernández Jaimes    Photography by Josephine Jael Jimenez

share with they agree. Everybody can connect to it because it's like we can all understand whether it's a minority, whether it's protesting or dealing with our president."

From a young age, he has experienced transformative beginnings that have resulted in being the man he is today. Born and raised in Colombia, Yeisson was adopted by his German dad when he was 11 years old and his name was changed to Jason. It was during his last years of high school that he decided to become someone new and name himself Jacquex. "That's the power of what you can do to set yourself to succeed. The main reason was that I'm a huge activist and I wanted myself to be clean, create a new person and reinvent myself. With me being Jacquex, I want to say that my goal in life is to leave the world a lot better than when I arrived in it. Being kind, bringing love back to our country, making the right changes," he shares.

At a young age, he already knew that he wanted to change the world and make a difference. With this powerful and striking name, Jacquex saw himself as a new palette to start fresh and begin the change with himself. He loves to dive into the arts and design. Jacquex doesn't permit himself to be limited to one thing, he's a designer that has studied fashion, nutrition, and business. His main goal is to work in the fashion industry, but Jacquex has found it very limited in terms of growth in the industry.

Upon studying business, Jacquex was able to understand the key roles it takes to be able to manage a business. He takes his passions and skills by working with lifestyle brands and helping them create a more inclusive social media strategy that not only showcases their products and values but provides a platform for representation.

# A loving,

compassionate and playful energy radiates and embraces you when having the honor of meeting Jacquex Frankel. He's a young Latino gay man that does all things with meaning, especially when he has a personal connection to a cause or person. Everything that he does, supports and shares is with his heart. You can count yourself lucky to be part of his circle. Be able to witness his passionate drive for a better, kinder world that doesn't have laws that restrict human rights.

"There's a standard base that queers are expected to succeed at everything. I think expectations are always there to exceed," Jacquex says. "We don't want to outdo each other, but progress in a way that is making changes that are great within our communities and outside of them. Being well rounded, I feel like that's the main goal for me as a gay person and being a minority. Coming from a third world country, these are the things that you kind of collect in your subconscious and are things you keep in mind. It's a lot of progressive change. I think that's something that within the queer community that I claim to. Everything that I do and support is with my heart and everybody I

"At some point in my life, my goal is to own a PR agency. Working with non-profit organizations for causes and things that need to be heard. I think a lot of it is that companies want to look good. They want to show that they're doing something good, but it's never really something that you hear about. There's not enough detail to making a brand image appear and look much more realistic than being just perfect. It's like a corporation. It's so built that there's no connection to it. I feel like companies have this well-designed business plan, it should include more progressive movements. That's definitely what I consider coming to the role," he announces.

He also shares about wanting to help artists and entrepreneurs share creative and analytical abilities to have their business grow. "I think when you open yourself to a wider spectrum of different mediums you can see differently. You're more realistic to the world of design," Jacquex says.

He also talks from experience. Jacquex has lived in Colombia, U.S., and Australia. He has been able to witness a wider spectrum of reality and be able to take what he's learned and incorporate it into his life.

"When I was there people were kind. Just anywhere you go, people would randomly talk to me, be nice. Everywhere you went it felt safe in a way. All the people that I met in Australia are very kind. Very big on politics, knowledge of what's going with the politicians. Big activists. I felt like I was in a group of people that was very much like me. It was very encouraging because this is another reason why I like to go to protests, because you can do so much through a social media platform, word of mouth, and when you go to these events or places with people like you, you remember you're not alone," Jacquex expresses. "This is just because you're doing it all the time alone, that it feels like you're not being heard. But when you decide to attend to these events it opens your mind to just be more independent and stand up for what you believe for. Australia was a place that I fell in love with, with the people."

""From Colombia, I think a third world country where you have no rights, you don't have freedom of speech. Terrorism is in the streets and poverty is everywhere. It's hard to make a living, I think it's eye-opening to see what possibilities you have if you get outside an environment that is toxic. You open doors for yourself when you make changes," he continues.

"Compared to the U.S. living in California, different areas, of course, you understand there are certain areas that are in their very own bubble. People don't accept gays, people who have no problem saying very discriminatory and stereotypical things that's mind-blowing for me! To be able to live in this state and to see something like that is happening, it upsets me a lot. This is the most progressive state like New York and we still have things like that going on and it's very interesting. I think it's realistic things and living in reality. Not be in a bubble."

"I think living in all those different countries in all different stages allowed me to at the right time support who I am. I've been able to witness things that have encouraged me to make a change. When I went back to Colombia and saw how realistic poverty is and all these issues, only encouraged me to be even more aware and raise awareness. And to be more outside of my box. Working and helping others. Put yourself first, but don't be selfish. That's one of my things I've been doing for the last traveling years that I've been able to experience," Jacquex shares.

As a young gay man, Jacquex also shares the discrimination he's faced in the United States and how ignorant

"Be a risk taker. Don't be afraid and be independent. The world is beautiful, you can trust the people around you. It takes one to know one. Be kind, it will come back to you. And the world is yours, go get it!"

insults can affect a young person. Seven years ago, he was visiting family in Dallas, Texas, and was approached by an older woman in a barbecue restaurant to insult him.

"She looked at me and said, 'Your kind of people are not welcomed here.' I was like, "What kind of people?" And she responded, "Gays." And I was just, "I don't understand." There was somebody that would say that to you. I immediately was infuriated that somebody had the guts to say that. That's so weird. She wasn't in her best health, so it was just really interesting to witness something like that. My cousin was just like, "don't engage, ignore it, it's not important. We're here to see our family, this is not our place." At the time, I wanted to say something," he says. "It was so unacceptable for her to say something like that to a young person. I think if they say it, someone who is of the same age, I think they would have a calm conflict, but when you say that to a younger human being that affects them even more."

"I remember coming back from the trip and wanting to be extra flamboyant. Anything that I wanted to be because no matter what anybody says, no one will change me. I'm going to do as I wish," Jacquex declares, "Isn't that the point of living? That you are here for you."

Verbal insults aren't the only thing Jacquex has faced. Stereotypes of his sexuality have made its way in his professional career as a stylist. He shares that he was chosen as the "Gay Consultant" to market idealistic clients. These experiences are the reasons as to why he wants to open his PR agency. He wants to work with companies and help break those stereotypes and discriminatory situations in the workplace.

"You can't assume that a gay guy is going to be a woman's best friend automatically. How stereotypical is that? When this happened at work, it was very interesting for me to understand that was the plan. This wasn't explained into detail. So when this happened, my main point when talking to my boss, I didn't feel comfortable doing this. It wasn't organic. The relationship didn't work with the business because that's what they wanted. I think overcoming things like that you either support that business in what they do or you don't," he continues. "And I didn't. It was like making a change and taking these life lessons and supporting what I believe in. Like buying a product, you know about the company, are you aware of what harm they're doing?" Jacquex also opens up about investing time for yourself and not allowing roadblocks of any kind overpower self-care. He opens up about not being able to attend protests and do things that he wanted due to timing constraints. Jacquex takes every life lesson as an opportunity to be more wise and selective of what and who he invests his time and ultimately be happy with.

# "Minority groups are always the ones who make a change."

"Always put yourself first and take care of you before anybody else. But at the end of the day for everybody not for an individual. With everything, I've been doing, with my projects, my friends, people who don't believe in the same ideals as you do then that's an obstacle. I think you can give someone the time and benefit of the doubt when they're coming with their best intentions. But if your political alignments don't work then it's really hard to keep that around. So I think a lot of it is being where you want to go, to be yourself, to keep being realistic, down to earth and being able to make changes. And people around you who support and believe in you will allow you. Just as there are ones that are an obstacle, there are the ones that are rewards that will help advance within yourself at the end of the day," he says.

Jacquex encourages young people to fight for the causes they believe in and to surround yourself with people that have the same mentality. For him making a change as a group is more progressive and an excellent way to understand more and helping you to not feel alone. He advises to also invest the time to learn and be more knowledgeable in politics. For him, it's not just about voting but to be aware of laws that are developing that will restrict people's bodies and rights. He also tries to balance self-care with knowledge and advises that the only way a person to make a difference is to also take care of their mental and health care.

"Minority groups are always the ones who make a change. It's like with what happened in Alabama trying to make abortion illegal. It's like who starts this protest and everything? The victims, the women. And within the gay community I think it's really important we're aware and on top of issues that are developing. Not only being well educated when it comes to voting," Jacquex continues.

"I think it's important to be well rounded in all different atmospheres. But also a lot of mental care, health care. Take in health awareness for {May} there's not even enough of awareness about that. People use apps for meditating, workouts, writing. Unless you're coming from a blue collar family, you don't experience therapies. You don't get to see other means of outlet and that's something really important," he says.

"People feel very alone, it's really important that's not the way people feel. When they wake up, they should feel loved and in an environment where they feel safe. If it's not in their home or in the country they live in, it will be somewhere else. They should go find it. Not to be afraid and be independent," he encourages. "Be a risk taker. Don't be afraid and be independent. The world is beautiful, you can trust the people around you. It takes one to know one. Be kind, it will come back to you. And the world is yours, go get it! This is our planet and for the next generation and we have a lot of work to put in."

# GENDER EUPHORIA

**YURA SAPI**

craving love
my love craving love
craving euphoria
trying to find it somewhere
failing
wasting the love on those who
cannot process it
those who waste it too
those who take but don't deserve

growing pains
like hair readjusting to its cut
feeling the same
but thinking back to what was before
thankful for being past
new concerns
new stressors
but ones in my control
and ones in front of me instead of held in my back
in the tension of my back

"I had my first crush on a boy when I was 11 and I was devastated.

At first, I could have sworn that I only liked him because he was nice to me... because he gave a damn about me while everyone else was tormenting me. But the butterflies in my chest, the tightening in my throat, the racing thoughts about his hair and his smile didn't fade and it killed me.

Growing up in conservative religious family, I was constantly told that being gay was a sin and I had to fight against the rights of gay people. I marched in the anti-LGBTQ+ rallies surrounding Prop 8 in California. I remember the hatred and disgust from my community, along with the repugnance from my mother. I listened as people told me that gay people are perverts and pedophiles; that the only thing worse than loving a man was killing one."

Anonymous

# twenty things i learned from you

Carlos García León

1.     I am queer.
    It was the moment you winked at me that
    Opened my eyes to the denial that I held on to so blindly

2.     Never date a coffee drinker.
    You'll never hear the end of how you should drink coffee
    Since it is one of two adult beverages

3.     Cuddling is so much better than sex.
    3.1 Especially if they have body hair.

4.     Sex is great with someone who has body hair.

5.     Sex, in general, is great.

6.     Coming out is so much easier when you are next to me.
    Because if no one is going to accept me, I know you will

7.     Hearing I love you is revolutionary.
    I never thought I would have someone
    Look at me, hug me, love me the way you do
    After years of being told I would never be able to

8.     You can fall in love more than once.
    I fell in love with the explorer, the musician,
    the guy who wanted to sleep after a few drinks,
    the beer drinker, the weed smoker,
    the man who has dreams to be a professor,
    the photographer, the cook,
    even the coffee drinker, the rugged guy with the biggest heart

9.  Showing affection is not a bad thing.
        Even though you neglected holding hands or hugging me
        You were uncomfortable to let people see your colors
        Or wanting to passionately kiss you in bed
        Because you cared more about sleep than me loving you

10. I can't read minds.
        You held on to your thoughts
        As if they were the reasons you were alive;
        Teaching me that silence and your presence was enough.
        Forcing to me to pry open your voice, making it so unreal;
        If you couldn't share your thoughts with me,
        your best friend and boyfriend,
        Who would you do it with?

11. Saying I love you is not the same as saying I'm sorry.

12. Saying I love you is not the same as saying I'm sorry.

13. Saying I love you is not the same as saying I'm sorry.

14. Realizing that we don't work out is harder
    and hurts more than breaking up.
        Living in the fiction that we've lived in
        ripping apart the story that we have created
        To realize that in reality I wasn't happy
        With the limits you had placed upon us
        Shatters my perception of what love is

15. Therapy is not necessary, but it certainly helps.

16. Moving on is easier when you have friends.
        Who are willing to tell you the truth
        That the person you are
        Wasn't the person you were
        When you were with him

17. You don't have to be friends.
        Even if you want to
        Because they've meant so much to you

18. I could have fallen in love with anyone, but I am glad it was you.

19. Drinking and dancing are good ways to have fun.
        And to forget you

20. Love isn't easy, love isn't hard, love is just love and I cannot wait to try
    again, for I am a better person now because of you.

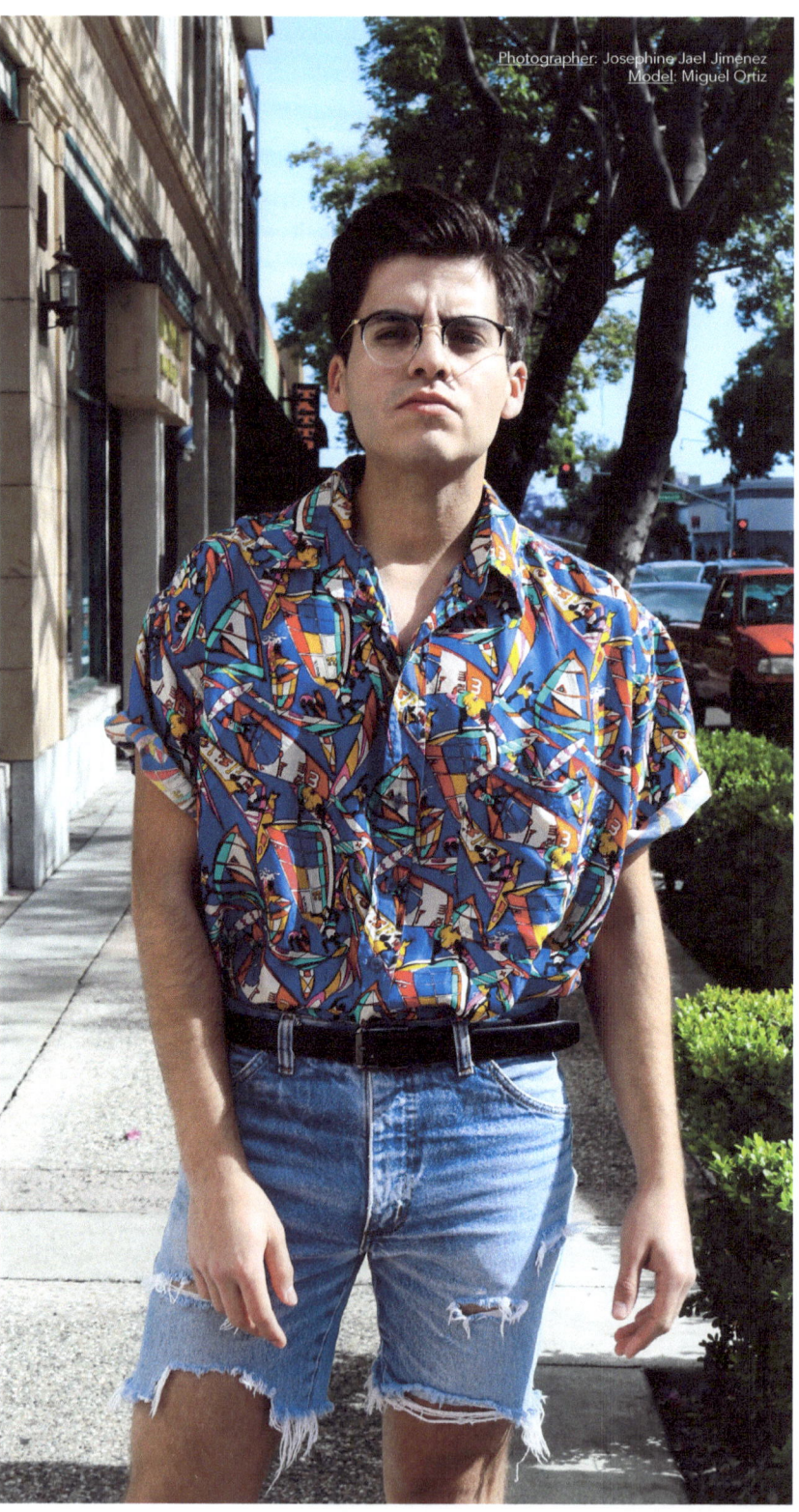

# Pride.

a playlist by TJ Meyer

JUNKY......................................................BROCKHAMPTON
Boobie Miles..............................................Big K.R.I.T.
Forrest Gump..............................................Frank Ocean
A BOY IS A GUN*.......................................Tyler, the Creator
Nakamarra..................................................Hiatus Kaiyote
Lucky Strike...............................................Troye Sivan
Know What I Want......................................Kali Uchis
Tears Dry On Their Own...............................Amy Winehouse
Animale Style..............................................Murs
HIM..........................................................Sam Smith
Take Me to Church.......................................Hozier
STAR..........................................................BROCKMAPTON
Big Wheels................................................Kevin Abstract
Tongue......................................................MNEK
Preach......................................................Keiynan Lonsdale
QUEER......................................................BROCKHAMPTON
Chanel......................................................Frank Ocean
All the Young Dudes....................................David Bowie
Steve Biko (Stir It Up)..........................A Tribe Called Quest
Don't Make Cents.................Proper Villains, Cakes da Killa
No Limits...................................................Angel Haze
SOMETHING ABOUT HIM......................BROCKHAMPTON
Fuck With Myself........................................BANKS
Honey......................................................Kehlani
My Favorite Shirt is My Skin...............................MOD SUN
i..............................................................Kendrick Lamar

# THEY ALL DO IT:
## Victorian Porn
## & Bisexual Women

LORRAINE RUMSON

It's hard to think of two fields that get more of a bad reputation for being anti-woman than Victorian England and porn.

Victorian England gets a bad reputation for keeping women passive and housebound, while porn gets a bad reputation for keeping women in bed with their legs open. One might assume that when Victorian stereotypes of women as passive mothers intersect with porn stereotypes of women as sexual objects, the result would be less than flattering.

While this may be the case for some of the pornography published in the nineteenth century, this assumption ultimately doesn't hold up. Due to being illegal across England, Victorian porn could not be regulated the way that "mainstream" publications could. The result is that Victorian porn presented shockingly liberatory (as well as generally shocking) stories of female sexual desire and power.

Nowhere is this more pronounced than in the anonymously published Lady Pokingham, or They All Do It, which was printed in the erotic magazine The Pearl between 1879 and 1880. Beatrice, the main character of Lady Pokingham, is a bisexual woman who ages from a precocious teenager to a mature adult over the course of the story's fifteen installments.

Female bisexuality in porn is not necessarily a sign that the porn is progressive. It can merely be the result of the fact that both heterosexual and lesbian porn are marketable for straight men. However, Beatrice displays an internal consistency in her desires for both women and men that indicates the story and author's respect for her sexual agency.

Beatrice's first sexual experience is with another girl at her school:

She seemed to take a great fancy to me, and the second night I slept with her (we had a small room to ourselves) she kissed and hugged me so lovingly that I felt slightly confused at first, as she took such liberties with me, my heart was all in a flutter, and although the light was out, I felt my face covered with burning blushes as her hot kisses on my lips, and the searching gropings of her hands in the most private parts of my person, made me all atremble. (Installment 1)

The girl in question, Alice, remains a presence in Beatrice's life until her marriage (in Installment 10). Alice acts as a role model for Beatrice in terms of how she explores and explains her sexual desire. She tells Beatrice the story of losing her virginity, including describing how her desire for a male servant in her household was mediated through her interest in the body of his female lover. Alice ultimately has sex with both the man and the woman, and uses her understanding of the woman's body as a means of explaining her desire to the man. Beatrice later uses this model when she has sex with men – including a liaison with Alice's brother (which Alice organizes).

Alice and Beatrice's relationship is a version of a common Victorian model of ideal female friendship. In novels like Charlotte Brontë's Jane Eyre or Jane Austen's Emma, deep emotional connections between women are understood as a key part of female life. The only difference with Beatrice and Alice, compared to Jane and Helen or Emma and Harriet, is that the emotional and practical support that they offer each other extends to sexual support as well.

The seven installments of Lady Pokingham that follow their meeting concern Beatrice's time as the centre of a polyamorous, multi-sexual web, primarily organized by and focussed on Alice. Beatrice's extensive experiences with both male and female sexual partners in this web present a sexual utopia in, which openness is rewarded with joy and love, while sex-negativity is punished (erotically, of course).

One could argue that Lady Pokingham's sexual openness only reiterates the same old straight-male fantasy of women being infinitely sexually available. However, Lady Pokingham does not fall into the common traps that make those fantasies potentially damaging. Beatrice and Alice are not empty vessels ready to be filled with penises or dildos, but rather characters with specific sexual wishes, and means of explaining and expressing those wishes to themselves and others. Despite (or because) it comes out of the illegal literature of Victorian England, Lady Pokingham, or They All Do It presents sexually active bisexual women with a respect for female-female relationships as well as female-male ones. It has taken feminist pornographers decades to reclaim this kind of openness to a variety of sexual experience, especially in venues that are meant mainly for men (as The Pearl was).

Lady Pokingham, along with the rest of The Pearl, has been digitized, and can be freely accessed on the website horntip.com (http://www.horntip.com/html/books_&_MSS/1870s/1879-1880_the_pearl_journal/) as well as purchased in hard copy or ebook from HarperCollins. While not all of the stories have the same sex-positive backbone, and even Lady Pokingham contains elements that are troubling (or even illegal) from a 21st-century perspective, reading them can offer a unique perspective on how to represent sexuality.

At the very least, it's a nice change from PornHub.

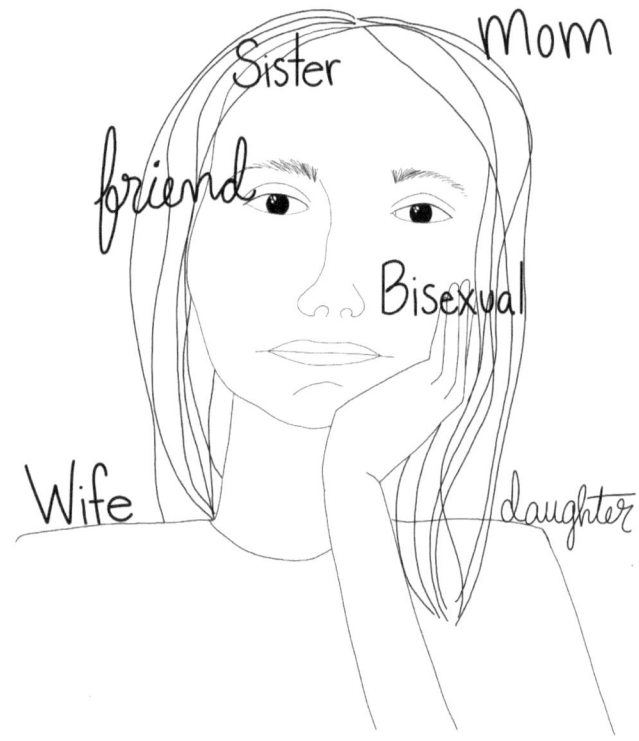

Illustration by Melissa Lee

Collective liberation

Means acknowledgement
Love
And action

New world order
Being in love with each other

Holding space for each other
Growth
Gratitude
Forgiveness
Listening

It's about addressing the true evils
And evils within

It's about figuring out how we can do this together

Beyond coexist
Coevolve
Colove

A better way to call in
A trust

Trust in solidarity

**YURA SAPI**

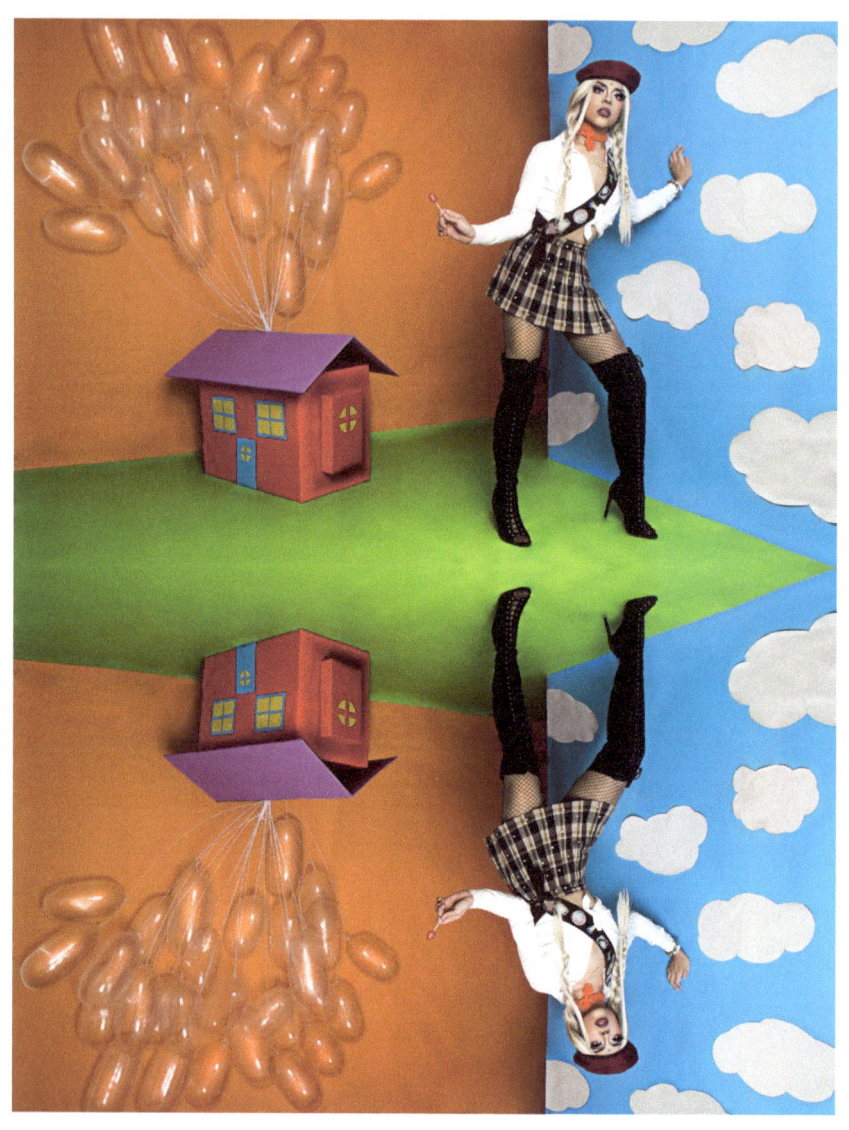

# MEET QUETZAL LUNA:
## YOUNG, FABULOUS AND ICONIC

Brenda Hernández Jaimes

Sugar, spice, and everything nice are just some of the many exceptional qualities that Quetzal Luna possesses. By daylight she's studying Chemistry at the National Autonomous University of Mexico (UNAM) - one of the best universities in Latin America and by night she's shining on stage. Quetzal is a young and intelligent trans Drag Queen with a bright future ahead who is inspired by pop culture such as UP, Sailor Moon and Cruella de Vil, and loves to exaggerate her image. Quetzal doesn't let anyone or anything stop her from living her stupendous life.

"I think we shouldn't label people. There are many people who don't know you can be transexual and a Drag Queen and they've been having this conflict that I used to have for a long time," she says.

Since she was very little, Quetzal wasn't happy with her assigned sex and the masculine treatment she was given. "I felt that something was missing. As if I wasn't complete. I was 15 years old when I discovered transgender and transexual people and I studied more about the subject. I identified a little and could possibly be a transexual person and want to change gender," Quetzal shares.

She continues on to sharing that she tried to live a life of the opposite gender and wearing more feminine clothes, but it wasn't completely fulfilling her. It wasn't until she discovered RuPaul's Drag Race on Youtube that she found her answer.

"I was astonished! I knew I wanted to do that for the rest of my life! I want to entertain people, recreate new fantasies whenever I want and people seeing me as an artist," Quetzal says happily.

She then went on to her first Drag Queen contest, Baby Drag held in Mexico City. Quetzal was filled with hope and gave herself the opportunity to see if it fulfilled and satisfied her then she would continue on that path and not look back, but if she didn't feel comfortable with what she was doing then she would continue looking for herself. Once she arrived, Quetzal was star struck and a bit intimidated by the rest of the Drag Queen participants.

"They all looked spectacular. I wasn't going to match their aesthetic, perfectionism and polished looks. I think life is always that way. When you enter something new, you feel a little intimidated, but I enjoyed it very much! I met a lot of my current friends there and this contest taught me so much. I had no idea what to expect and it helped me polish myself," she declares.

Quetzal might have not won the title of Baby Drag, but she discovered that being a Drag Queen was her calling and that it made her finally feel complete. It's only been a year and three months since the contest, but she knows this will be her life and she doesn't see herself stopping anytime soon. The competition has encouraged her to see Drag as a form of artistic expression and an extension of who she is that sets her free to provide a twist to beauty.

"For my Drag, I didn't want to create a fictional character. I want to use all my essence and personality because I feel that at some point when creating a fictional character I would end up losing myself in it. My essence and image are a bit more exaggerated," Quetzal explains.

She goes on to share that she hasn't encountered many obstacles, but as a trans person prejudices have been part of her life. Her family and school were prejudiced of the path she had chosen. They all thought she would quit high school and not be able to attend the university she had wanted. For a time that had stopped her from moving forward, Quetzal didn't want to disappoint her family and was afraid of other people's opinions of her. But when there's a will, there's a way and she demonstrated to everyone that it was possible to graduate from high school, get accepted to UNAM, study chemistry and be a Drag Queen.

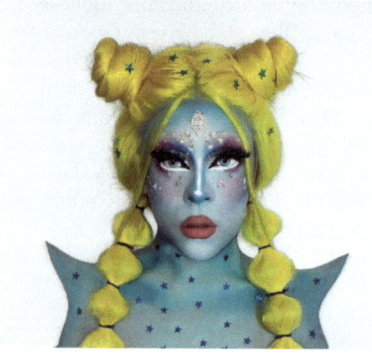

"Everyone would say to me that most Drag Queens didn't have a degree and only worked in bars. But I knew that I didn't want that for myself. I told them I can study, have my job and my hobby! I can handle all three things and I dedicate enough time to each one. I wanted to have this duality and I've been able to achieve it," she states proudly. "Drag is all about making fun of all the rules that exists and have been imposed by society and make people see that we can change certain things that are wrong. We can provide awareness of our way of living and keep everyone in check," she continues and also opens up about her transition.

"At first my transition was difficult. I had many doubts if I was either transsexual, drag or transvestite. I was also having problems of not being able to find myself. I needed to do something. It was a bit difficult, but once I could be both, drag and transsexual, there's no limit to myself

and I didn't want to label myself to only one thing. I told myself, 'I'm going to accept myself, I'm going to take care of myself and I will not care what other people think of me."

"My mom was one of the first people that I was afraid to [tell] because I was afraid of disappointing and letting her down or have her worry about me. My mom is the only person whose opinion about me is important and the one she has isn't bad!"

Quetzal shares that her mother and brother support her decisions and explains that even though later on her father gave his support, he told her he didn't like what she was doing.

"He never wanted to see me dressed like a woman, have a wig and wear heels. But over time, he's been accepting and he's trying to educate himself so he can talk to me, ask what's happening. So my parents support, but my mom supports me 100%," she says.

Quetzal might be only 18 years old, but she knows she has a responsibility to her current and future generation of fellow trans people who want to follow into her sparkly footsteps of being a Drag Queen. She wants to make people realize that there aren't limits to Drag. Her goal is to expand on the word and break the rule that in order to be part of the Drag community, one has to imitate the opposite gender.

"Drag isn't an imitation. You can be Drag and trans. It's your way of expressing your art. Do not limit yourself to anything," she advises to her fellow trans youth, "Let yourself experiment with anything you want. Don't judge yourself ahead of time and let yourself be carried away by your feelings, emotions and artistic side. Because it's so beautiful," Quetzal continues, "At the beginning you'll see many barriers that society has imposed on you: your family and school. Making you be the same as everybody else...you can never compare yourself to anyone. Always

keep in mind that you are you! You are the only one who has your essence and no one will be the same as you. Try not to compare yourself with others, but do elevate yourself. With the same qualities and characteristics that you have, work them and don't try to imitate others. Try to be you and live," Quetzal encourages.

She also talks about the negative connotations that Drag Queens have in Mexico. It's not about vices, sex or alcohol and Quetzal discourages those stereotypes and prejudice. Drag Queens can go to school and shine both on stage and off. What she does take in mind are the criticisms when she's on stage.

"Criticism is more difficult than the pain your body experiences. There are people who know how to handle it and others who don't. Those are the people that collapse and stop doing it. I think it's important to take all those criticisms and build yourself with all of it," she says.

As for what she envisions for herself this year, Quetzal's mission is to appear on the YouTube reality show competition, La Más Draga 3. Although it's a secret on how participants win their spot on the show, it's well known that the most famous Drag Queens of Mexico City are personally invited to be part of the competition.

"I have about a year to prepare so that I can show people the best version of myself. It's going to be a difficult year because I'm going to work a lot to to be able to make myself be noticed and be part of La Más Draga."

A star has been born and Quetzal has demonstrated time again that she can accomplish the goals she sets for herself. Her light has just begun and it wouldn't be any surprise to see her win the coveted spot and inspire a young trans teen to begin their own shiny path.

# Queer Adventures in Ecuador

## Quito -
So many queer adventures! Our highlights are the lesbian @TouchUIO discotecas and @DirtySanchezBar where we met another lovely chicx, @almendelmar96_11.

## Baños -
We met a (straight) couple at the thermal baths and went on a double date after running into them again in town searching for a place to eat.

## Guayaquil -
Along the malecón boardwalk there is a famous statue of two men shaking hands. Their stature and manner of being suggests to locals that they may have been a little more than professional acquaintances... Of course, we had to get a picture of ourselves in front of it standing in the exact same pose.

## Montañita -
Only 2 hours after arriving we hear, "Chicas, happy brownies?" Yes, this is the beach of happy brownies and where our blog name comes from. It's a laid-back surfer town during the day and a wild hub for party life at night. Highly recommend.

## Manta -
This place was just about the two of us spending quality time together and treating ourselves to some good things. We went to the movie theater, spent days lounging on the beach, and went out to a nice restaurant with a beautiful view.

## Atacames -
Here just about everyone is Afro-ecuadorian (unless you're a tourist). While on the beach, someone asked for help with her son's English homework. One of her friends was "lesbiana" and asked us about our relationship. We learned about "activa y pasiva" vocabulary.

## Tena -
On our way out of Tena, we got stopped by the transit police. While searching our things, they accidentally turned on one of our vibrators and didn't know how to make it stop. The situation turned from slightly terrifying to pretty hilarious. In the end, they ended up stealing the vibrator! (We assume this was a bribe in their minds.) #queeradventures

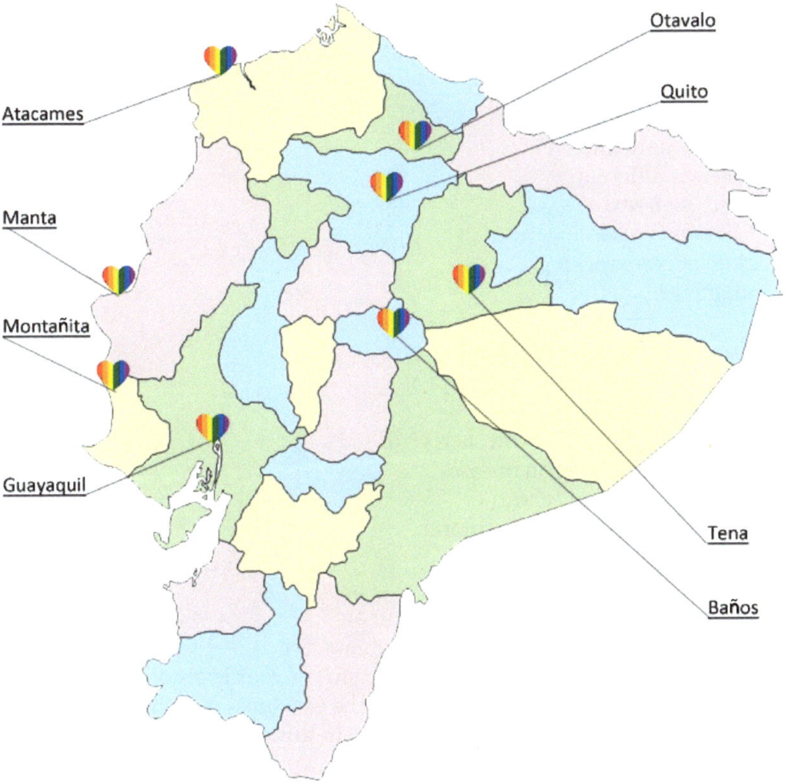

Otavalo

Quito

Atacames

Manta

Montañita

Guayaquil

Tena

Baños

COURTESY OF

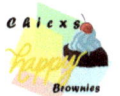

Read more about their adventures on
Medium, Patreon, and Instagram
@ChicxsHappyBrownies

# BABE

## CARLOS GARCÍA LEÓN

I had only been with one man
Before this moment,
But this was different.
That had been sex,
But this was...
Exciting, nerve-wracking...
Lovemaking?

I had seen you shirtless before.
It wasn't the first night we had slept at
Each other's sides,
But pulling off your shirt with such vigor
As your put your hands on my ass
And your mouth on my chest;
Your torso was a new Greek sculpture
That had just been discovered.

I broke that stone beauty as I pushed you on
My bed. Finding your lips with an easefulness that
Comes from awkward attempts. Struggling to get your jeans off.
Not even Michelangelo could have gotten the exactness of your
Waist down. You bounced back, taking lead in this dance
As you stepped forward to unbutton my pants.

The hair on your beard tickling me as your tongue pressed against mine
While your arms pulled on my underwear, the same elasticity that we share in
This pattern of attraction, being rather teasingly away and extremely pressed on.
The smell of your armpits than secreted a husk of a man that drove me wild
As I explored down the hair on your chest to find your nipple with my tongue.
It was just the beginning of an adventure, because the trail kept going south.
Temptation reaches its max when you are only wearing one piece of clothing.

It feels that I have an army to beat before I can finally see you in the glory
That Greek gods would hide to mortal eyes.
I start removing your tight underwear
From behind, caressing your butt with tremors
because I'm not sure I can handle the sight.
Perhaps I am a demigod because I am surviving, but barely breathing,
Seeing you fully naked, shining in the blissfulness that is you.

There are no words that can describe the sensation that
Comes from being inside you, or you inside me.
Many have tried, and my attempt still cannot
Paint the feeling that makes me moan in
Ecstasy, or grab the sheets as if I were
Holding myself from falling in
A cliff. It's love, in the rawest
Form of the word.

We end,
Together.
Covered in sweat
Your torso pulsing,
Struggling to adapt
To the amount of fluids
Seeped out.
This is my first time
Making love
Let's do it many more times.


And we do.

**Brenda Hernández Jaimes**, Editor and Head Writer, @bren_jai
**Carlos García León**, Contributor, @cgarcia_leon
**ChicxsHappyBrownies**, Contributor, @chicxshappybrownies
**Jacquex Frankel**, Model, Interviewee, @thecooljag
**Joey Reyes**, Issue Consultant, @joeykangaroooooo
**Josephine Jael Jimenez**, Editor & Designer-in-Chief, @josietakestheworld
**Lorraine Rumson**, Contributor, @its.lorraining
**Melissa Lee**, Contributor, @thehouseoflees
**Miguel Ortiz**, Model, @miguelortizo
**Quetzal Luna**, Model, Interviewee, @quetzal.lv
**TJ Meyer**, Contributor, @admeyertj
**Yura Sapi**, Contributor, @yurasapi
**Young Ignorantes**, @youngignorantes, www.youngignorantes.com